T0401660

VOLUME 1

ADVENTURES IN ACTS

Written by
DAVID LUCKMAN

Illustrated by
SILVANA DI MARCELLO

CF4•K

10 9 8 7 6 5 4 3 2 1

Copyright © 2024 David Luckman

ISBN: 978-1-5271-1018-2

Published by Christian Focus Publications,
Geanies House, Fearn, Tain, Ross-shire, IV20 1TW, U.K.
www.christianfocus.com

Illustrations by Silvana Di Marcello
Design by Pete Barnsley (CreativeHoot.com)

Printed by Imprint Press, India

All words in bold are included in the glossary at the end of volume 2.

THIS BOOK BELONGS TO:

_____

CONTENTS

ACTS

The Book of Acts is history. It was written
by Luke who also wrote Luke's Gospel.

Acts is all about what Jesus did after he went
back to heaven.

In the Book of Acts, Luke tells us about the spread of the
good news about Jesus all over the known world, and the
beginning of his church.

Luke wants God's people to be certain that the good
news about Jesus is truly God's message and to know
how to live for Jesus until he comes back again.

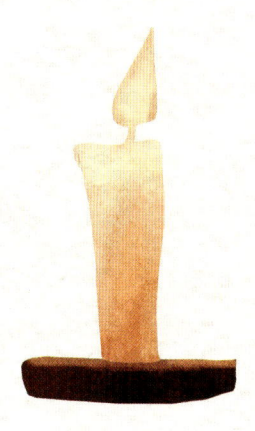

BACK TO HEAVEN

Acts 1:1-12

Dear Theophilus, in my first book I wrote about everything that Jesus began to do and teach until the day he was taken up to heaven. Just before he went into heaven, and by the power of the Holy Spirit, he gave instructions to the men he had chosen as his **apostles**. After his death and resurrection, Jesus showed himself to these men for forty days, proving to them that he was alive and teaching them about the Kingdom of God. On one occasion he was eating with them, and he gave them a command: 'Stay in Jerusalem and wait for the gift that my Father promised to give you, which I told you about. John baptised with water, but in a few days, you will be baptised with the Holy Spirit.'

When the apostles met with Jesus, they asked him, 'Lord, are you going to restore the kingdom to Israel now?'

Jesus answered them, 'It's not for you to know the times and dates set by the authority of my Father. But when the Holy Spirit comes upon you, then you will receive the power that you need to be my witnesses in Jerusalem, and in all Judea and Samaria, and to the ends of the earth.'

After Jesus said this, he was taken straight up into heaven before their very eyes. A cloud hid Jesus from their sight.

They were still looking up at the sky when two men clothed in white garments stood beside them. 'Men of Galilee,' they said, 'why are you standing here looking up into the sky? This Jesus, who has been taken from you into heaven, will come back in the same way that you have seen him go.'

WHAT'S THE POINT:

Luke tells us about the earthly life and ministry of Jesus until the day he was taken back to heaven. In his second book, called Acts, Luke tells us of the *continued* ministry of Jesus. Jesus still teaches and works from heaven. Jesus does this through his Holy Spirit and the apostles teaching the gospel. We also learn of the importance of the **church** in God's plans for his world. His followers must tell the whole world about the good news of Jesus Christ before Christ's return.

LOOK BACK:

Read Isaiah 44:3-8

'You are my witnesses...' Jesus speaks the same words to his followers that God spoke hundreds of years earlier to the nation of Israel. By doing this, Jesus is telling the apostles, and the world, that he is God and Lord of all.

CHECK THIS OUT:

Read Luke 24:13-48

Luke provides some details of what happened during those forty days after the resurrection of Jesus.

THINK

Why is it so important that Jesus went back up to heaven? Read John 15:5-11 to get you started.

A PLAN THAT CAN'T BE STOPPED

Acts 1:12-26

The apostles went back to Jerusalem from the Mount of Olives. It is approximately one kilometre away from the city. They entered the city and went to the room where they were staying. In the room were Peter, John, James and Andrew, Philip and Thomas, Bartholomew and Matthew, James the son of Alphaeus, Simon the Zealot, and Judas son of James. They all joined together constantly in prayer, along with the women and Mary the mother of Jesus, and his brothers.

It was during this time that a group of **disciples** gathered in Jerusalem. There were about 120 of them. Peter stood up to speak and said, 'Brothers and sisters, the Scripture had to be fulfilled. The Holy Spirit spoke long ago about Judas Iscariot through the mouth of King David. Judas was a guide for the group who arrested Jesus. He was one of us, and he shared in this work.'

(Judas bought a field with the money he got for his evil deed. When he was in his field, he fell to the ground. His body burst open, and his bowels spilled out. Everyone who lived in Jerusalem heard about it. In their own language they called it *Akeldama*, which means 'Field of Blood.')

Peter continued, 'For it is written in the Book of Psalms, "May his house be abandoned, let no one live in it." It also says, "may someone else take his place as a leader." Therefore, it is necessary to choose someone to join us. He must be one of the men who went with us as we travelled about with the Lord Jesus, starting from John's baptism until the day that Jesus was taken up into heaven. He must become a witness with us of the resurrection of Jesus.'

Two names were put forward: Joseph who was known as Barsabbas (also known as Justus), and Matthias. Then they prayed,

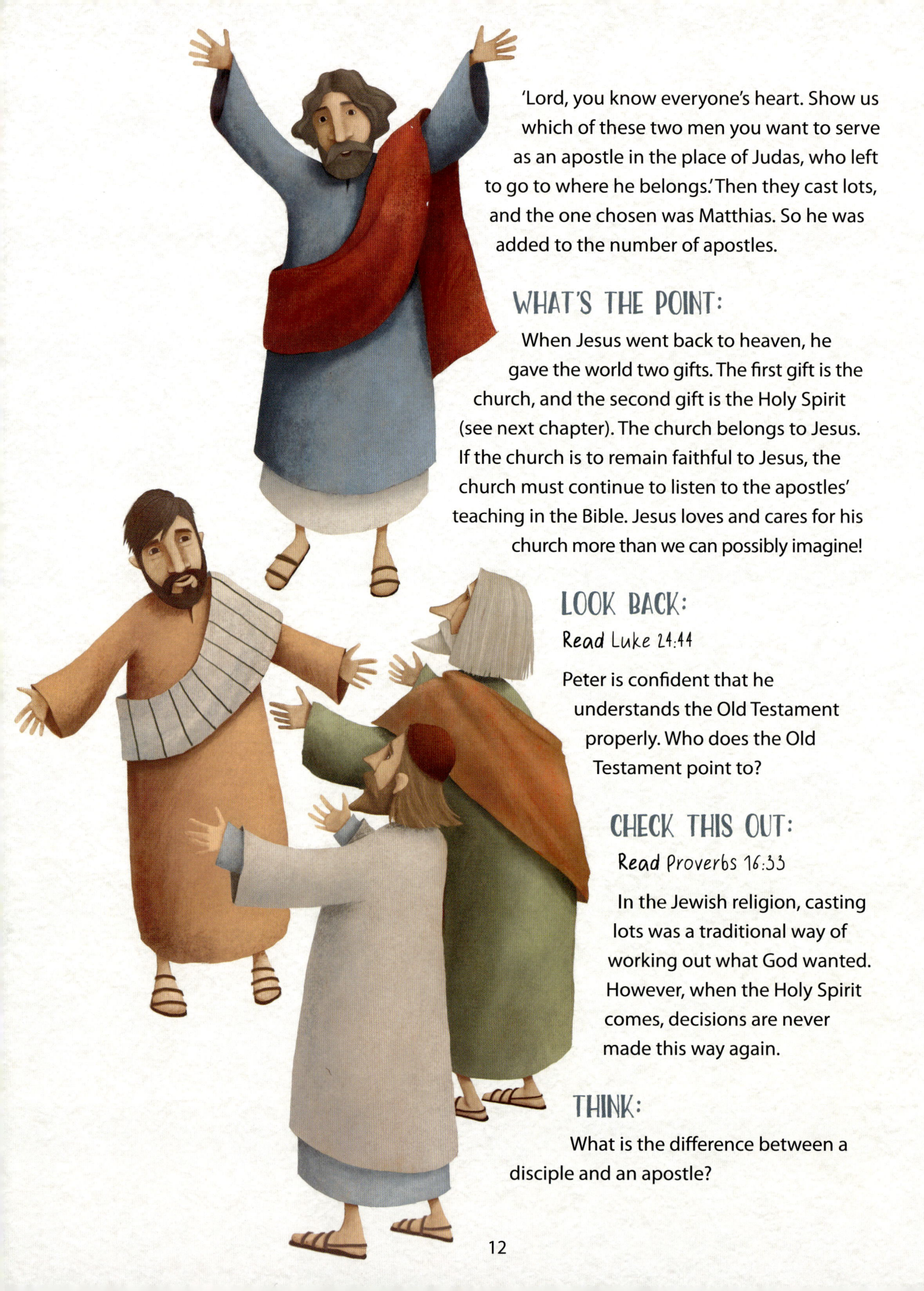

'Lord, you know everyone's heart. Show us which of these two men you want to serve as an apostle in the place of Judas, who left to go to where he belongs.' Then they cast lots, and the one chosen was Matthias. So he was added to the number of apostles.

WHAT'S THE POINT:

When Jesus went back to heaven, he gave the world two gifts. The first gift is the church, and the second gift is the Holy Spirit (see next chapter). The church belongs to Jesus. If the church is to remain faithful to Jesus, the church must continue to listen to the apostles' teaching in the Bible. Jesus loves and cares for his church more than we can possibly imagine!

LOOK BACK:

Read Luke 24:44

Peter is confident that he understands the Old Testament properly. Who does the Old Testament point to?

CHECK THIS OUT:

Read Proverbs 16:33

In the Jewish religion, casting lots was a traditional way of working out what God wanted. However, when the Holy Spirit comes, decisions are never made this way again.

THINK:

What is the difference between a disciple and an apostle?

THE PROMISE COMES
Acts 2:1-13

The Day of **Pentecost** came. The disciples of Jesus were all together in one place. Suddenly, they heard a loud noise. It sounded like a wind. But it was not a wind. It was the power of God coming down from heaven to the place where the disciples stayed. It filled the whole house. Then they saw little pillars of fire, like tongues, resting on them. Each of the disciples was filled with God's Holy Spirit. They started to speak in languages that they did not know. The Holy Spirit was helping them do this.

God-fearing Jews had come from every nation to Jerusalem for the harvest celebration. They heard the disciples speaking in languages that were not their own.

The crowd was confused. They heard the disciples speaking in each of their own languages. How could this be? All the disciples were from the area of Galilee. How could they speak to the people in their own languages? It was amazing!

There were Parthians, Medes, and Elamites. There were people who lived in Mesopotamia, Judea and Cappadocia. There were people from Pontus and Asia, Phrygia, and Pamphylia. There were people from Egypt and parts of Libya near Cyrene. There were visitors from Rome, Cretans, and Arabs. All the people said, 'We hear these people declaring the wonders of God in our own languages! What does this mean?'

Others made fun of the disciples. 'They have had too much wine to drink!' they exclaimed.

WHAT'S THE POINT:

Jesus Christ went back into heaven. The Holy Spirit came. God's people began to speak the good news about Jesus Christ. The Holy Spirit has come to point all people to Jesus, to put God's Word in our hearts and to bring us into a new family, called the church. The Holy Spirit helps us to know God as our Father, and Jesus Christ as our Saviour and Lord.

LOOK BACK:

Read Ezekiel 37:1-14

There is a valley of dead dry bones. As God's Spirit enters the dead dry bones, they become alive. It was a picture of when God will pour out his Spirit and create his church. It pointed to this Day of Pentecost when the Holy Spirit came.

CHECK THIS OUT:

Read Genesis 11:1-9

At Pentecost, God reversed the curse at Babel. God divided the people at Babel because of their sin and rebellion against him. But at Pentecost, God brought the people together because of Jesus and his gospel.

THINK:

Why is the coming of the Holy Spirit at Pentecost a wonderful and important moment in history?

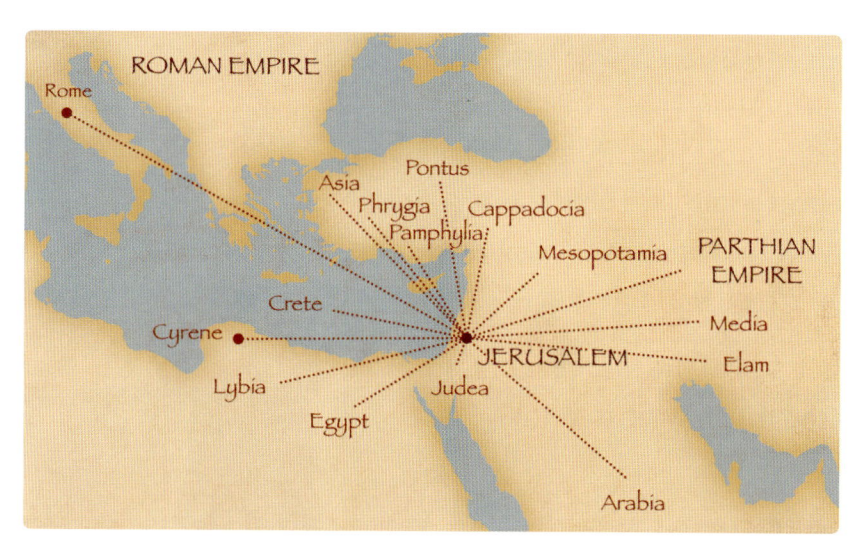

REPENT AND BELIEVE
Acts 2:14-47

Peter stood up with the other eleven apostles. He raised his voice and spoke to the crowd that had gathered. 'My fellow Jews, and all of you who live in Jerusalem, listen carefully and I will explain what is happening. You may think that these men are drunk, but they are not. It is only nine o'clock in the morning! But this is what God said would happen, through his **prophet** Joel: 'In the last days, I will pour out my Spirit on everyone. Your sons and daughters will prophesy; your young men will see visions and your old men will have dreams. In those days, I will even pour out my Spirit on my servants, both men and women, and they will prophesy. I will show wonders in the heavens above and miraculous **signs** on the earth below. There will be blood, fire, and clouds of smoke. The sun will be dark, and the moon will turn red as blood. This will happen before the coming of the great and glorious Day of the Lord. And everyone who calls on the name of the Lord will be saved."

Peter then told them of Jesus Christ, the Son of God.

'God has raised this Jesus to life, and we are all witnesses of the fact,' he said. 'Jesus has been raised to the right hand of God, his Father, and has received from him the Holy Spirit.

What you see and hear now is the gift whom he promised. Let all the people of Israel know that this Jesus, whom you crucified, is both Lord and Christ.'

Those who listened carefully and received his word, repented of their sins, believed, and were baptised. God added about three thousand people to the number of the church that very day.

The disciples of Jesus faithfully followed the teaching of the apostles and enjoyed fellowship together. They broke bread with each other and prayed together constantly. Everyone was filled with awe and many miracles were done by the apostles. Those who followed Jesus shared everything they had with each other. They sold their possessions and divided the money between all the people, depending on the need of each person. Every day they met at the temple. They ate together in their homes with glad and sincere hearts, praising God and enjoying the good will of all the people. And as they told others the gospel of Jesus every day, the Lord added to their number those who were being saved.

WHAT'S THE POINT:

The risen and ascended Lord Jesus Christ continues to teach and act from heaven as the gospel is preached by the apostle Peter. The crowd does not understand what is going on, but as Peter explains the gospel of Christ to them, the Holy Spirit opens their eyes to help them see who Jesus is and how they should respond to him.

LOOK BACK:

Read Joel 2:28-32

The book of Joel is a call from God to his people to turn back to him. It is a book about God's judgement of all people everywhere. And there is only one who has the power and purity to judge the world on the 'Day of the Lord.' Who does Peter say it is?

CHECK THIS OUT:

Read Psalm 16:8-11 and Psalm 110:1

King David spoke these words about a thousand years before Peter's sermon. He was not speaking about himself. Do you know who King David was talking about in these verses?

THINK:

How should you respond to the gospel of Jesus Christ?

EVEN BETTER THAN GOLD
Acts 3:1-10

One day Peter and John were going up to the temple. It was three o'clock in the afternoon. It was time for people to gather for prayer. There was a man who was crippled from birth and could not walk. Every day he was carried to the temple gate which was called Beautiful. He begged people for money as they entered the temple.

When the beggar saw Peter and John about to enter the temple courts, he asked them for money. Peter and John looked directly at him. Then Peter said to the man, 'Look at us!' He looked at them expecting to get some money from them. Then Peter said, 'I do not have any gold or silver. But I will give you what I have. In the name of Jesus Christ of Nazareth, get up and walk.'

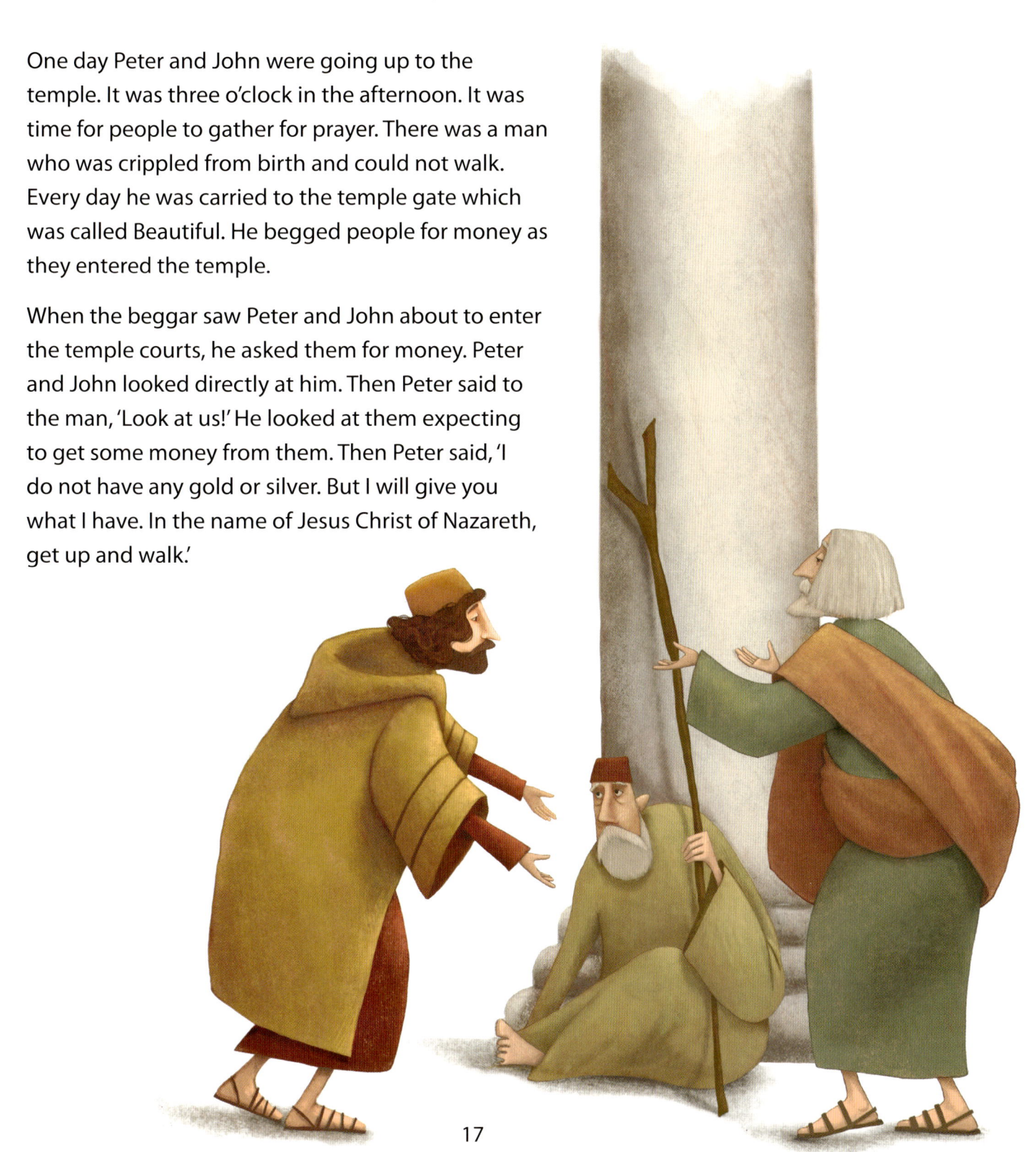

Peter grabbed the man's right hand and helped him up. Straight away the man's feet and ankles were strong. He leapt up and started to walk. He walked into the temple courtyard with Peter and John. As they walked together, the man jumped into the air and praised God.

The people saw the man walking and leaping and praising God. They knew it was the beggar who sat at the temple gate called Beautiful every day begging for money. The people were amazed. They were filled with awe at what had happened to him.

WHAT'S THE POINT:

A sign points us in the right direction. This miracle points us in the right direction to Jesus. It points us to the day when Jesus Christ will return to make everything new. The lame beggar shows how weak our bodies can be. We get sick, we grow frail, and we die. Through Peter and John, the Lord Jesus healed this man immediately and completely. This miracle is a sign of what heaven will be like.

LOOK FORWARD:

Read 1 Corinthians 15:42-44

Your earthly body is weak, sinful and will only last for your time on earth. But your heavenly body will be strong and brilliant. It will be the perfect body for living in heaven with Jesus forever.

CHECK THIS OUT:

Read Deuteronomy 15:7-11

Why did God tell the people of Israel to have no beggars in their midst?

THINK:

There was a crippled beggar at the Beautiful Gate in the temple of Jerusalem, right at the very heart of Israel! What do you think went wrong in Israel for this to happen?

TRUST IN JESUS

Acts 3:11-26

The healed beggar held on to Peter and John. All the people were amazed. They ran to them in the place called Solomon's Porch. When Peter saw this, he said to them, 'Men of Israel, why are you surprised at this? Why do you stare at us? We did not make this man walk by our own power or godliness. The God of our fathers, the God of Abraham, Isaac, and Jacob, has done this. God has brought glory to his servant Jesus. You handed Jesus over to be killed. You denied you knew Jesus before Pilate, even though Pilate had decided to let him go. You disowned Jesus, the Holy and Righteous One. You demanded that a murderer be set free instead of Jesus. You killed Jesus, the one who gives life. But God raised Jesus from the dead. We are witnesses of this. And this man whom you see and know, has been made strong through faith in the name of Jesus. It is the name of Jesus and the faith that comes through him, that has healed this man completely as you can all see.

Now brothers and sisters, I know that you and your leaders acted in this way because you did not know Jesus. Long ago God said through his prophets that his **Messiah** had to suffer. And it happened as God said it would. Therefore, repent and turn back to God, so that your sins may be forgiven. If you do this, times of refreshing will come from the Lord to you. He will send Jesus Christ, who has been chosen for you. He must stay in heaven until it is time for God to restore everything. He promised this long ago through his holy prophets. Moses said, 'The Lord your God will send you a prophet like me. He will be from your own people. You must listen to everything he tells you to do. Anyone who does not obey him will be separated from God's people.' All the prophets since the time of Samuel, spoke of these days. You are all heirs of the prophets and of the **covenant** which God made with your ancestors. He said to Abraham, 'Through your children, I will bless all the peoples on earth.' When God raised his servant Jesus, he sent him first to you, to bless you by turning every one of you away from all your evil ways.'

19

WHAT'S THE POINT:

The resurrection of Jesus brings refreshment and restoration to his people. The resurrection of Jesus wipes out our sins. We are declared forgiven by Jesus. We know that the truth refreshes us today because we have the assurance of restoration and eternal life that Jesus gives us. So we rejoice that Jesus is risen and trust him with our lives.

LOOK BACK:

Read Isaiah 35:5-6

The Old Testament prophet Isaiah said that God's Messiah would come to restore the world. The restoring of the beggar's feet and ankles is a preview of the future restoration of the whole creation by God.

THINK:

Around two thousand years ago, a lame man was completely restored to health, in the name of Jesus. Even today, medical science cannot do this. How do you explain that?

SPEAK UP
Acts 4:1-22

As Peter and John spoke to the people, the priests and the captain of the temple guard and the Sadducees came up to them. They were angry that the apostles taught the people and preached the resurrection from the dead through Jesus. They arrested Peter and John. As it was evening, the two men were put in prison until the next day. However, many who heard the Word of God believed and the number of men grew to about five thousand.

The next day the rulers and elders and teachers of the law, along with Annas the high priest, Caiaphas, John, Alexander and as many who were of the family of the high priest, gathered in Jerusalem. They had Peter and John brought before them to answer their questions. 'By what power did you do this? In whose name did you do this thing?' they demanded.

Filled with the Holy Spirit, John answered them. 'Leaders and elders of the people! If we are being questioned today about an act of kindness shown to a lame man and how he was completely healed, then you should know, and so should all the people of Israel, that it is by the name of Jesus Christ of Nazareth, whom you crucified but whom God raised from the dead, that this man stands before you today.

Jesus Christ is "the stone you builders rejected but is the most important of all." Salvation is found in Jesus Christ alone. There is no one else whom God has given who can save us.'

When they saw how brave Peter and John were, and realised that they were ordinary uneducated men, they were amazed. They took note that these two men had been companions of Jesus. There was nothing they could say because they could see the man who had been healed standing there with Peter and John. They sent the men out of the room so they could confer with each other. 'What shall we do with these men? It is clear to everyone living in Jerusalem that a notable miracle was done by them. We cannot deny it. But to stop it spreading any further, we must warn these men not to speak any longer in the name of Jesus.'

They called the men back in and ordered them not to speak or teach anymore in the name of Jesus. But Peter and John said to them, 'Whether it is right in God's sight to listen to you than to God, you judge for yourselves. We can only speak of the things that we have seen and heard.'

They threatened Peter and John some more and then they let them go. They could not find a way to punish the men, because the people were all praising God for what had happened to the lame man. It was a miracle because the man who was healed was over forty years old.

WHAT'S THE POINT:

This is a war between human authority and God's authority. Peter and John are brought before the same men who executed Jesus. They are not worried about the truth. Instead, they ask by what authority did Peter and John speak? Peter and John had a choice – to be silent or to boldly speak up about Jesus. They obeyed Christ and chose to speak up! Jesus wants us to obey him and speak up!

LOOK BACK:

Read Psalm 118:22

The capstone was the most important cornerstone that kept a building from falling down. For the psalmist, the capstone was Israel's king, the one who would keep the nation of Israel from crumbling. For Peter, Jesus is the capstone in God's building which is the church. If they try to build a religion for Israel without Jesus, their building will crumble. God will not be part of it. Rejecting Jesus means rejecting the *only* hope of salvation that God offers.

CHECK THIS OUT:

Read Matthew 5:11-12

As Jesus Christ is risen and God is in control of his world, then we have the freedom to speak and to be bold for Jesus.

THINK:

If someone in authority told you to do something that is against the will of God, what would you do?

GOOD TO PRAY

Acts 4:23-31

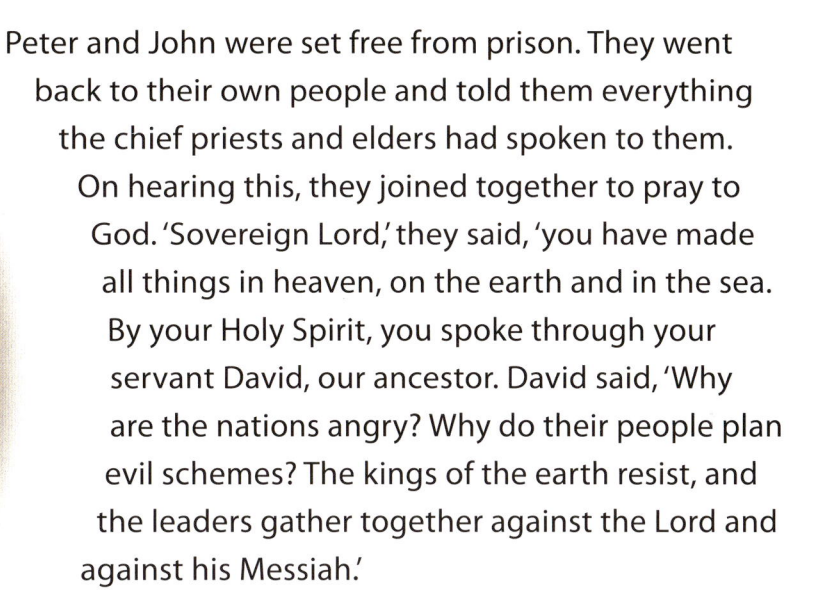

Peter and John were set free from prison. They went back to their own people and told them everything the chief priests and elders had spoken to them. On hearing this, they joined together to pray to God. 'Sovereign Lord,' they said, 'you have made all things in heaven, on the earth and in the sea. By your Holy Spirit, you spoke through your servant David, our ancestor. David said, 'Why are the nations angry? Why do their people plan evil schemes? The kings of the earth resist, and the leaders gather together against the Lord and against his Messiah.'

'In fact, Herod and Pontius Pilate met together with the Gentiles and the Israelites in this city. They gathered together to plot against your holy servant Jesus, the Messiah. They did what you wanted them to do. So now, Lord, consider their threats. Help us, your servants, to speak your word boldly. Stretch out your hand to heal and perform miracles through the name of your holy servant Jesus.'

When they finished praying, the place where they were gathered started to shake. They were all filled with the Holy Spirit and began to speak the Word of God, boldly.

WHAT'S THE POINT:

As soon as Peter and John were set free, they went back to the fellowship of disciples. The first thing they did was pray. God is in control of his world. They did not ask God for a quiet life. They prayed for boldness to keep speaking the gospel of Jesus (which was the thing that got them into hot water in the first place!) God wants us to be faithful and to take comfort that he is in complete control of his world today. God wants us to boldly tell people about King Jesus too.

LOOK BACK:

Read Psalm 2

Although there is opposition to God's Messiah from kings and nations, he will reign forever. The apostle Peter tells us that this psalm is pointing to Jesus Christ, who is God's Messiah. And he will reign forever!

CHECK THIS OUT:

Read Isaiah 45:9 and Romans 9:20-21

The Bible says that God is sovereign. That means there is no one or nothing greater than God. He is in complete control of his world. He made it. He made everything and everyone in it. God rules over all. He is in charge; he's the boss.

THINK:

What is the first thing you do, when you are suffering or feeling anxious and afraid?

SHARE TOGETHER

Acts 4:32-37

All the disciples were of one heart and mind. No one claimed to own anything, but they shared everything with each other. With great power and authority, the apostles kept telling people about the risen Lord Jesus. And God blessed them all greatly. No one had any needs among them. Occasionally someone who owned land or property sold them and gave the money from the sales to the apostles, laying it at their feet. Then it was given out to others according to their needs.

There was a Levite from Cyprus called Joseph. The apostles also knew him as Barnabas (which means Son of Encouragement). He sold a field that he owned. He brought the money to the apostles and gave all of it to them.

WHAT'S THE POINT:

There was outward evidence of the change in heart and mind. Now that the disciples belonged to God, there was a new attitude towards the things they owned. There was also a new generosity when certain needs arose among the family of God. The Holy Spirit nurtures a deep and supernatural oneness in the hearts and minds of the disciples of Jesus.

LOOK FORWARD:

Read 2 Corinthians 8:1-7

The Holy Spirit changes our attitude to the things that we own, so that we are willing to share everything we have with others who belong to God's family.

THINK:

Is there a Christian brother or sister at church who is in need? What can you do to help?

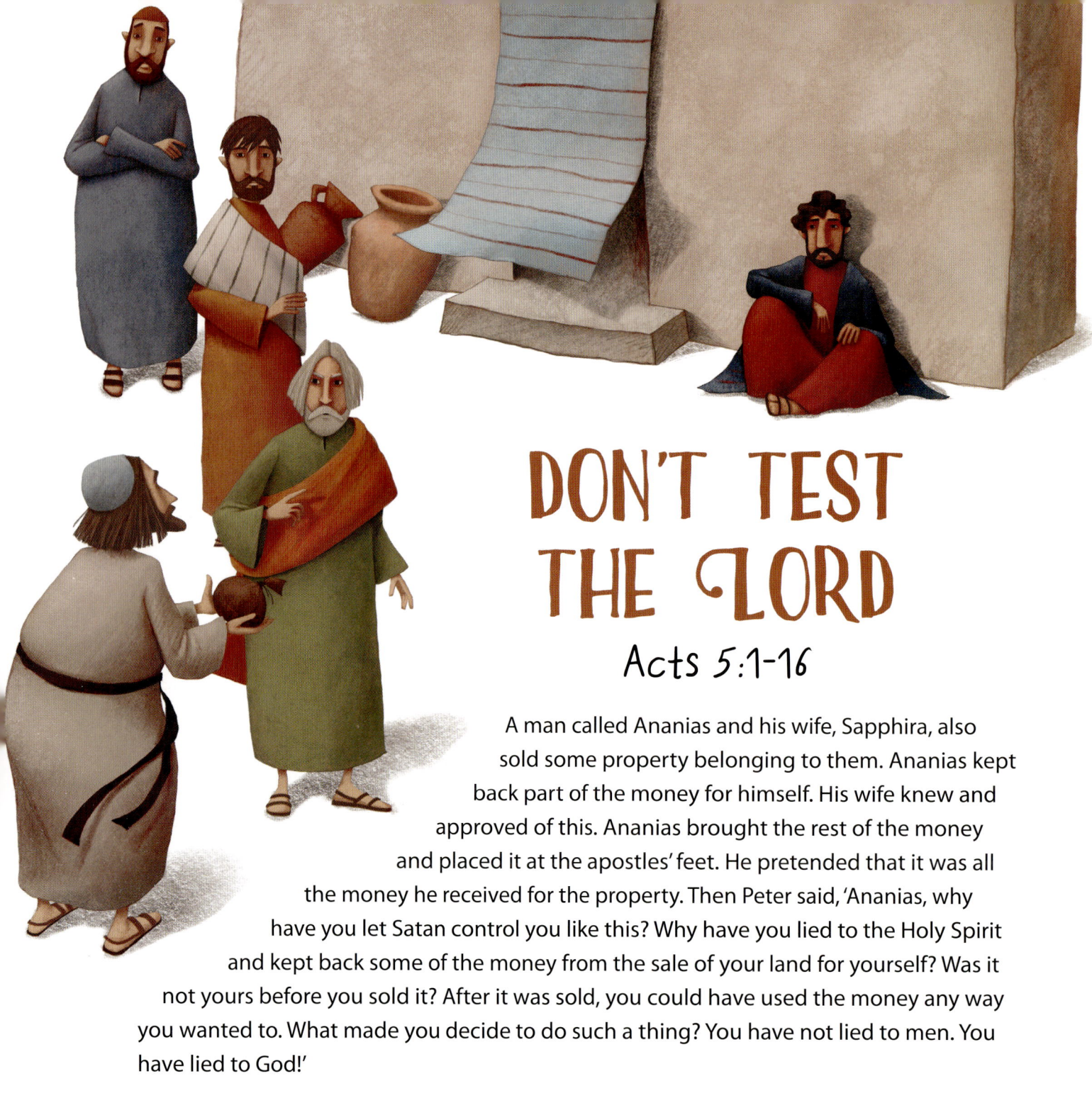

DON'T TEST THE LORD

Acts 5:1-16

A man called Ananias and his wife, Sapphira, also sold some property belonging to them. Ananias kept back part of the money for himself. His wife knew and approved of this. Ananias brought the rest of the money and placed it at the apostles' feet. He pretended that it was all the money he received for the property. Then Peter said, 'Ananias, why have you let Satan control you like this? Why have you lied to the Holy Spirit and kept back some of the money from the sale of your land for yourself? Was it not yours before you sold it? After it was sold, you could have used the money any way you wanted to. What made you decide to do such a thing? You have not lied to men. You have lied to God!'

When Ananias heard this, he fell down dead, and great fear gripped those people who heard everything that happened. Then some young men came and wrapped up his body. They carried him out and buried him.

About three hours later, the wife of Ananias arrived there. She did not know what had happened. Peter asked her, 'Tell me, is this the amount you got for selling your property?'

'Yes,' she replied, 'that is the full amount.'

Then Peter said to Sapphira, 'Why did you decide to test the Lord's Spirit? Look! The men who carried your husband outside to bury him are at the door. They will do the same thing for you.'

Immediately Sapphira fell down dead at the feet of Peter. The young men came in and found her dead. They carried her out and buried her next to her husband. The whole church, and all who heard about these events, were really frightened.

The apostles did many miracles among the people. All the believers used to meet together in Solomon's Porch. Although the people thought well of them, nobody dared to join their number. Still, more and more men and women believed in the Lord and did join their group in the end. Because of this, people brought their sick friends and family into the streets and put them on beds and mats on the ground. They hoped that Peter's shadow would fall on them as he walked by. Crowds of people from the towns around Jerusalem came to the apostles. They brought the sick and those tormented by evil spirits with them. All of them were healed.

WHAT'S THE POINT:

Ananias and Sapphira saw some wealthy believers being generous with their possessions and money. They saw the joy and admiration that their generosity brought. Ananias and Sapphira decided to sell a property they owned, but they held back some of the money. They gave the money to the apostles pretending it was everything. They wanted respect in the community. They wanted to look good. Ananias and Sapphira thought they could get away with lying to the apostles, but they could not get away with lying to God. Their deaths are a sign of God's judgement on their hypocrisy. God hates hypocrisy in his children.

LOOK BACK:

Read Joshua 7:1-26

The people of God were moving into the land God promised them. Their journey was stopped because Achan stole something that belonged to God. In the same way Ananias and Saphira stole something that belonged to God. They were also punished for their actions.

CHECK THIS OUT:

Read 1 Corinthians 3:16-17

God does not live in a building. God lives in his people, the church. God loves his church. His church is to be holy. God acts against anyone who would destroy the growth of his church.

THINK:

Why is the church so important to the Lord Jesus Christ?

FACING OPPOSITION
Acts 5:17-42

The high priest and the Sadducees were jealous of the apostles. So, they had the apostles arrested and put into jail. An angel of the Lord appeared to them during the night. The angel opened the prison doors and brought them out. Then the angel said, 'Go and stand in the courts of the temple. Tell everyone the full message of this new life.'

At dawn, they went into the temple courts just as they were told to do. They began to teach the people the truth about Jesus Christ.

When the high priest and his companions arrived, they called a meeting of the Jewish ruling council, also known as the Sanhedrin. They sent word to the prison to have the apostles brought before them. When the officers arrived at the prison, they could not find the apostles there. They went back and reported, 'We found the prison securely locked and the guards were standing at the doors, but when we opened them, we could find no one inside!' When the chief priests and captain of the temple guard heard this, they wondered what could have happened to the apostles.

Then someone came and told them, 'The men you put into jail are standing in the courts of the temple teaching the people the Word of God.' Hearing this, the captain of the temple guards took some of his officers with him to fetch the apostles from the temple courts. However, they did not use force because they were afraid that the people might stone them.

They brought the apostles to appear before the high priest and the Sanhedrin. They were questioned by the high priest. 'We told you clearly not to teach in the name of Jesus,' he said. 'Now it seems that you have filled all Jerusalem with your teaching. And you are telling everyone that we are responsible for his death!'

Peter and the other apostles replied, 'We must obey God, not men! The God of our forebearers raised Jesus from the grave. You killed him by nailing him to a cross. God raised Jesus to his right hand as Prince and Saviour, that he might offer repentance and forgiveness of sins to the people of Israel. We are witnesses of these things. So is the Holy Spirit whom God has given to those who love and obey him.'

When the Sanhedrin heard this, they were furious and wanted to kill the apostles. A member of the Sanhedrin was called Gamaliel. He was a Pharisee and teacher of the

law. He was well respected by the people. He stood up and ordered that the apostles be removed from the meeting and put outside for a little while. Once they were gone, he spoke to the members of the Sanhedrin. 'My fellow Israelites,' he said, 'think carefully about what you are going to do to these men. You remember some time ago, Theudas came along claiming to be an important man and about four hundred people followed him. He was killed and all his followers cleared off and nothing more happened. Then there was Judas from Galilee. He appeared during the days of the census. He led a small group of people in a violent protest but was killed and all his followers ran away too! So, let me advise you to leave these men alone! Let them go! If their activity is of their own making, then it will fail. But if it is from God, you will not be able to stop them. In fact, you will be fighting against God if you do try to stop them.'

The Sanhedrin were convinced by Gamaliel's words. They called the apostles in and **flogged** them. Then they ordered the apostles to stop speaking in the name of Jesus and released them.

The apostles left the Sanhedrin. They were overjoyed because God had deemed them worthy to suffer disgrace for belonging to Jesus. Every day in the courts of the temple, and in people's homes, they never stopped teaching and proclaiming the good news that Jesus is the Messiah.

WHAT'S THE POINT:

The Sanhedrin refused to believe in Jesus because they were proud and jealous. Belief in Jesus as the Messiah threatened their power and authority over the people, especially as they saw many joining the church every day. So, they **persecuted** and threatened the apostles. This did not stop the apostles from speaking about Jesus and suffering for it. The apostles counted it a privilege to be treated as their Master had been treated. We will also face hostility from others who do not want to believe in Jesus.

LOOK BACK:

Read Luke 9:23-26

You can't have it both ways. You can't follow Jesus and live your life any way you want. Carrying your cross is another way of saying you are following Jesus or you have surrendered your life to Jesus.

CHECK THIS OUT:

Read Matthew 27:62-28:15

There are similarities between the resurrection of Jesus and the prison release of the apostles. Can you see what they are?

THINK:

What does it cost to be a Christian?

REJECTING GOD

Acts 6 and 7

The apostles chose seven men to help them in their daily work. One of these men was called Stephen. He was a man full of faith and the Holy Spirit. He did great wonders and miracles among the people. Some members of the **synagogue** argued with Stephen. But they could not stand up to his wisdom and the words the Holy Spirit spoke through him. They had a secret meeting and persuaded some men to tell lies about Stephen. 'We have heard him say evil things against Moses and against God.'

So, the people, the elders and teachers of the law became agitated. They seized Stephen and brought him before the Sanhedrin. They brought false witnesses in to say, 'This man never stops saying wicked things against this holy place and the Law of God. We have heard him say that this Jesus of Nazareth will destroy this place and change the customs that Moses gave us.'

All who sat in the Sanhedrin looked closely at Stephen. They saw that his face was like the face of an angel.

Then the high priest asked him, 'Are these accusations true?'

Then Stephen said, 'Listen to me, men of Israel. God does not live in temples built by hands. As the prophet said, "Heaven is my throne, and the earth is my footstool. What house will you build for me?" says the Lord. "Or where is the place of my rest? Have I not made all things?"

'You stubborn people! Your hearts are hard! Your ears are closed! You are just like your ancestors: you always fight against the Holy Spirit! Which of the prophets did you not treat cruelly? They even killed those who spoke of the coming of the Righteous One. And you have betrayed and killed him. You received the Law from angels, but you have not obeyed it.'

When the Sanhedrin heard this, they were filled with anger and ground their teeth at him. However, Stephen was full of the Holy Spirit. He looked steadily up to heaven. He saw the glory of God. He saw Jesus standing at the right hand of God. He said, 'Look! I see heaven open. I see the Son of Man standing at God's right hand!'

When they heard this, the members of the Sanhedrin covered their ears. They cried out with a loud voice. Then they ran at Stephen. They dragged him out of the city and stoned him. The witnesses took off their cloaks and placed them at the feet of a young man called Saul.

As they stoned Stephen, he prayed, 'Lord Jesus, receive my spirit.' He knelt down and cried out, 'Do not count this sin against them.' Then he died.

WHAT'S THE POINT:

Time and again the Israelites rejected the messengers that God graciously sent them. They were sent to call the people of Israel to turn back to God – to love and obey him. Stephen reminded them of this terrible rejection. The climax of their rejection was rejecting the Son of God, Jesus Christ. They nailed him to a cross. People still reject God and his Son, Jesus.

LOOK BACK:

Read Isaiah 66:1-2

God does not need buildings. They are not special to him. What is really important to God is that you love him, and trust and obey his Word, the Bible.

CHECK THIS OUT:

Read Exodus 32:1-35 and Deuteronomy 18:15

God sent Moses to rescue his people. In the wilderness, the Israelites challenged his authority. They did not listen to Moses. They turned away from God and rejected his rescue. But God promised to send another rescuer like Moses. His name? Jesus.

THINK:

Christians must warn people not to reject God. Are you willing to stand up for Jesus, whatever the cost?

HEAD-TO-HEAD

Acts 8:1-25

Persecution broke out against the church in Jerusalem. All those who served the Lord Jesus ran away to find safety in the towns and cities of Judea and Samaria. Only the apostles stayed in Jerusalem. Some godly men buried Stephen. They were deeply saddened by his death. Meanwhile, a man called Saul tried to destroy the church. He went from house to house, looking for anyone who loved and served Jesus. When he found them, he dragged them off to prison.

The believers who had left Jerusalem, evangelised as they went on their way. Philip went to a city in Samaria and began to speak to the people there about Jesus Christ. The crowds saw the miracles he did, and they listened carefully to what Philip said. Evil spirits came out

from many people with loud shrieks. Many paralysed and lame people were healed. So, the people in the city were full of joy.

There was a man called Simon who lived there. He was a magician. The Samaritans were amazed by his sorcery. He boasted that he was a great man! Everyone gave him their attention, from the most important people in the city, to the least important people. 'Simon has power from God!' they exclaimed. The people followed him because he had astounded them for such a long time with his sorcery. However, as Philip preached the good news about Jesus Christ and the Kingdom of God, many men and women believed and were baptised. Simon believed and was baptised too. He followed Philip around the city. When Simon saw Philip performing many miracles and signs, he was amazed.

The apostles heard that the people of Samaria believed the Word of God that was preached to them. They sent Peter and John to visit them. When the two men arrived, they prayed for the people, that they might receive the Holy Spirit, because he had not come upon them yet. They had only been baptised in the

name of the Lord Jesus. Then Peter and John placed their hands on them, and the Holy Spirit came upon them.

Simon saw that the new believers received the Holy Spirit when the apostles lay their hands on them. So, he offered Peter and John money. 'Give this power to me too, so that anyone upon whom I lay my hands, may also receive the Holy Spirit.'

However, Peter exclaimed, 'May you and your money perish for believing that you can buy God's gift with money! You have no part or share in this ministry because your heart is not right with God. Repent of this evil and pray to the Lord, that he might forgive you for thinking this way. I can see that you are a harsh person and a prisoner to sin.'

Simon replied, 'Please pray to the Lord for me, so that none of the things you spoke of may happen to me.'

Peter and John gave their testimony and proclaimed the Word of the Lord. Then they returned to Jerusalem, evangelising in many Samaritan cities on the way.

WHAT'S THE POINT:

It took persecution to drive the early Christians out of Jerusalem. God used the persecution there to advance the gospel of Christ to Samaria. Many people stopped following Simon the Magician. Now they lived with Jesus Christ as King of their lives. All this was part of God's plan to draw men and women, boys, and girls, into his family. People's lives are transformed when they hear and believe the gospel of Jesus Christ.

CHECK THIS OUT:

Read Matthew 10:5 and John 4:9-26

Jews hated Samaritans and Samaritans hated Jews! The church in Jerusalem would find it extremely difficult to believe that any Samaritan could be a true believer. The Holy Spirit was held back from the believers in Samaria so that Peter and John could see the truth for themselves – that the believing Samaritans were indeed genuine Christians too. God showed his full acceptance of the Samaritans by giving them his Holy Spirit.

THINK:

What can you do to reach the community that you belong to with the good news of Jesus?

THE MESSAGE SPREADS

Acts 8:26-40

An angel of the Lord told Philip, 'Go south to the desert road that leads from Jerusalem to Gaza.' So, Philip did as he was told. On his way, he met a man from Ethiopia. The man was an important official who looked after the wealth of Candace, the queen of Ethiopia. He had travelled to Jerusalem to worship God at the temple. On his return, he was sitting in his chariot reading from the book of the prophet Isaiah. The Holy Spirit said to Philip, 'Go to that chariot. Stay close to it.'

Philip did what he was told. He ran up to the chariot. He heard the man reading from the book of the prophet Isaiah. 'Do you understand what you are reading?' asked Philip.

'How can I understand it. I need someone to explain it to me,' replied the Ethiopian. 'Come up and sit next to me,' he said. Philip did as he was told.

The Ethiopian official was reading this passage in the book of the prophet Isaiah:

'He was led like a sheep to be killed,
and as a lamb is silent before the removal of its wool,
so he did not say a word.
He was shamed and not allowed any justice.
No one can talk about his descendants,
because his life on earth was cut short.'

The Ethiopian asked Philip, 'Who is the prophet talking about? Tell me please. Is it himself, or someone else?'

Starting with that passage from the book of the prophet Isaiah, Philip told the Ethiopian the good news of Jesus Christ.

As they travelled, they came to some water. The Ethiopian said, 'Look, it is some water. Why should I not be baptised?' He ordered his chariot to stop. Philip and the Ethiopian got out of the chariot. They went down into the water and Philip baptised the Ethiopian official. When they came up out of the water, the Spirit of the Lord took Philip away. The Ethiopian official never saw him again. He continued his travels, and he was full of joy. Meanwhile, Philip reappeared at Azotus. He travelled all around the area. He preached the good news about Jesus in all the towns until he arrived at Caesarea.

WHAT'S THE POINT:

God led Philip to speak to an Ethiopian government official about the good news of Jesus. This man came to believe in Jesus as Lord and Saviour. He was baptised. He became part of the family of God, even though he was from a faraway country.

He was also not a Jew. God wants all people, everywhere, to know and understand the gospel of Jesus. God has commissioned his children to speak the Word of God to people who are lost without him.

LOOK BACK:

Read Isaiah 53: 4-11

The prophet Isaiah tells us that the Servant of God suffered when he did not deserve it. Philip explained to the Ethiopian that the passage he was reading in Isaiah was pointing to Jesus. It was all about Jesus, God's suffering Servant. Jesus suffered though he did not deserve it. Jesus suffered because of what his people did wrong.

CHECK THIS OUT:

Read Philippians 2:6-8

Not only did the Lord Jesus come among us as God's suffering Servant – not only did he lay down his life for sinners, but he chose to be executed on a cross! Because Jesus died in our place and for our sins, justice is done, and mercy is poured out freely on everyone who receives it by faith in Jesus.

THINK:

Will you explain the good news of Jesus to someone who does not understand it?

A SURPRISING CHANGE

Acts 9:1-19

Saul continued to make murderous threats against the disciples of Jesus. He went to the high priest and asked him for letters to the synagogues in Damascus. He wanted permission to find men and women who belonged to the **Way**. He wanted to bring them back to Jerusalem as prisoners to be punished. At about midday, Saul was near the town of Damascus when a bright light from heaven, stronger than the

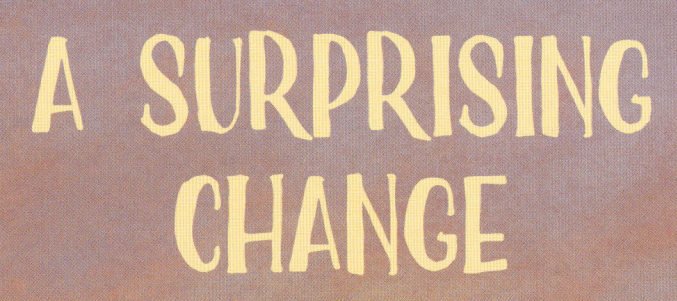

sun, shone around him. He fell to the ground. He heard a voice saying, 'Saul, Saul, why do you persecute me?'

'Who are you, Lord?' asked Saul.

'I am Jesus,' replied the Lord. 'I am the one you are persecuting. Get on your feet and go into the city of Damascus. When you get there, you will be told what to do.'

The men who travelled with Saul were lost for words. They heard the voice, but they did not see anyone. Saul got up from the ground. When he opened his eyes, he could not see. So, they led him by the hand into Damascus. He was blind for three days. He did not eat or drink for the whole time he could not see.

There was a disciple of Jesus living in Damascus. His name was Ananias. The Lord spoke to Ananias in a vision and said, 'Ananias!'

'Yes, Lord,' answered Ananias.

'Go to the house of Judas,' the Lord told him. 'You will find the house on Straight Street. Ask for a man from Tarsus called Saul. He is praying. In a vision, he has seen a man named Ananias come and place his hands on him to restore his sight.'

Then Ananias said, 'Lord, I have heard many bad things about this man. He is a wicked man who has hurt your people in Jerusalem. And he has come here with the authority of the chief priests to arrest all those who love and serve you.'

'Go!' the Lord commanded Ananias. 'I have chosen this man to carry my name before the Gentiles and their kings. He will bring my name before the people of Israel too. I will show him how much he will suffer for my name.'

Ananias did what the Lord told him to do. When he found the house on Straight Street, he went in. He placed his hands on Saul and said, 'Brother Saul, the Lord Jesus appeared to you on the road as you were coming here. He has sent me so that you may receive your sight and be filled with the Holy Spirit.'

As soon as Ananias said these words, it was as if scales fell from Saul's eyes. He could see again. He got up and was baptised. When he had eaten some food, he was stronger. He stayed on for some days with the disciples in Damascus.

WHAT'S THE POINT:

Ananias thought Saul could never change because his heart was so full of hatred for Jesus and his people. But *Jesus forgave him!* Saul's change from a wicked man to a servant of Jesus brings hope to everyone. No matter how bad someone is, Jesus can change and restore them into his family, like he did Saul.

LOOK BACK:

Read Isaiah 59:9-10

Hundreds of years before, the prophet Isaiah spoke of personal blindness that keeps everyone away from God. And at Pentecost, murderous Saul stumbled in darkness at midday as though it were the dark of night. It is a picture of his life. Saul knew a lot about the Jewish religion, but everything he knew did not lead him to put his faith in Jesus Christ as God's Messiah.

CHECK THIS OUT:

Read John 15:18+20 and 2 Corinthians 11:24-29

Jesus said to Saul, 'Saul, Saul why do you persecute me?' Any attack on Jesus's followers is an attack on Jesus. Following Jesus can bring pain and persecution. The world hates Jesus and anyone who serves him.

THINK:

Can you think of someone that you feel doesn't deserve to be forgiven and changed by Jesus? What does God say about that? Read Psalm 103:11-12 and 1 John 1:8-9 to get you started.

A COMPLETE CHANGE
Acts 9:19-31

Saul stayed the with disciples for a few days. Straight away he went into the synagogues and started telling the people about the good news of Jesus. He told them, 'Jesus is the Son of God.' Those who heard Paul were amazed at him. They said, 'Is this not the man who caused fear and grief in Jerusalem, going after those who called on the name of Jesus? Surely the reason he is here is to find them, bind them, and deliver them to the chief priests?' But Saul grew stronger every day. He proved that Jesus was the Christ to the Jews who lived in Damascus. They could find no words to answer him.

As the days went by, the Jews came up with a plan to kill Saul. Day and night they watched the city gates to see if he would pass through them, so that they could kill him. However, his followers learned of this plot. One night they took Saul to an opening in the city wall. They lowered him in a basket through the wall onto the ground beneath.

Then Saul made his way to Jerusalem. He tried to join up with the disciples of Jesus in that city, but they were afraid of him. They did not believe that Saul was a true Christian. So, Barnabas took Saul to the apostles. He told them of Saul's journey along the road to Damascus. He told them that Saul had seen the Lord

Jesus on the road, who spoke to him. Barnabas spoke of how Saul had preached the good news of Jesus fearlessly in Damascus.

Saul was allowed to stay with the believers in Jerusalem. He proclaimed the gospel of Jesus with courage, to all who would listen. Saul even debated with the Greek-speaking Jews there. But they wanted to kill him too. The believers found out about this. They brought Saul to Caesarea, and from there they sent him to Tarsus.

At that time the church throughout all of Judea, Galilee, and Samaria lived in peace. The Holy Spirit comforted and strengthened the church, which grew in numbers. And all those who believed in Jesus, worshipped him wherever they went.

WHAT'S THE POINT:

Saul carried the name of Jesus to the Gentiles. He also suffered for doing it. Telling someone the good news of Jesus can bring terrible hostility. But there is no opposition too great for God. He can turn even the most savage opponent into a preacher of the gospel. So, trust God. His plan to spread the good news in all the earth cannot be stopped.

LOOK BACK:

Read Matthew 5:10-12

Jesus tells us of the way that the world will respond to his followers. If you know what it is to face hatred and opposition because of your love for Jesus, 'rejoice and be glad, for your reward is great in heaven'.

CHECK THIS OUT:

Read Galatians 1:13-20

It was three years from when Paul met Jesus Christ to when he went to Jerusalem. During that time, he preached the good news about Jesus in Arabia and Damascus. When he went to Jerusalem, the believers there were most suspicious of him. Do you think they were right to feel that way about Paul? If not, why not?

THINK:

Would you be surprised if God was working in the heart and mind of someone that you are afraid of, or has made your life difficult?

TIME TO GET UP
Acts 9:32-43

Peter went about the country. He wanted to visit the followers of Jesus in Lydda. He found a man called Aeneas there. This man could not walk. He had stayed in bed for eight years. 'Aeneas,' said Peter, 'Jesus Christ heals you. Rise up and make your bed.' Aeneas got up straight away. The people who lived in the town of Lydda and the surrounding area of Sharon saw what had happened to Aeneas. They put their trust in the Lord.

There was a believer called Tabitha who lived in the coastal town of Joppa. She was also called Dorcas. She was a kind person who was always doing good deeds and helping those who were poor. Around the same time that Peter was in Lydda, Tabitha got sick and died. Her friends washed her body and placed it carefully in a room upstairs. Lydda was not too far away from Joppa. When the followers of Jesus in Joppa heard that Peter was close by in Lydda, two of them were sent to get Peter. 'Please come immediately!' they begged him.

Peter went with the two disciples to Joppa. When he got there, he was quickly taken upstairs to the room where Tabitha lay. Many widows stood crying around Peter. They showed him the beautiful robes and clothes that Tabitha had made for them while she was alive.

Peter sent everyone out of the room. When the room was clear, he got on his knees and began to pray. He turned to the lifeless body of Tabitha. 'Tabitha, rise up,' he commanded. She opened her eyes and looked at Peter. Then she sat up. Peter took her by the hand and helped her onto her feet. It was a miracle! Peter called out to the believers and widows to come back into the room. He showed them Tabitha who was alive. All the people of Joppa heard about this. Many of them put their trust in the Lord. Peter stayed for a while in Joppa. He lived at the home of Simon the **tanner**.

WHAT'S THE POINT:

The healing of Aeneas and raising of Tabitha are little thumbnail pictures of the wonderful salvation that Jesus brings. Both were beyond human help. But only Jesus saved them. Many put their trust in the Lord and followed him.

LOOK FORWARD:

Read Hebrews 2:1-4

The miracles the apostles did were signs that the message of Jesus, they proclaimed, was true. So, when the apostles tell us that God wants to forgive us our sins, if we repent and trust in his Son, Jesus Christ, then we can believe it!

CHECK THIS OUT:

Read John 20:9

When Peter tells Aeneas and Tabitha to *rise up*, he uses the same word that speaks of God *raising* Jesus from the dead. When we say sorry for our sins, and place our faith in Jesus, he forgives us our sins and he *raises us up* to new life!

THINK:

Do these miracles remind you of any others?
Read Luke 5:17-26 and Luke 8:40-56. Jesus told the man and the girl to *rise up*. Peter used Jesus's words. Can you think why he did that?

A BIG OBSTACLE

Acts 10:1-23

In the town of Caesarea there lived a soldier called Cornelius. He was a commander in the Italian Regiment. Cornelius was a religious man. He and his family feared God. He generously gave his money away to people in need and he prayed to God all the time. One day at about 3 o'clock in the afternoon, Cornelius had a vision. He saw an angel of the Lord who came to him and said, 'Cornelius.' Cornelius was afraid. He looked at the angel. 'What is it, Lord?' asked Cornelius.

'God has heard your prayers and seen your acts of generosity to those in need. God will remember this,' said the angel. 'Now send some of your men to the city of Joppa. Tell them to bring Simon who is also called Peter back here to you. He is staying with a man called Simon who is a tanner. His house is by the sea.'

The angel then left Cornelius. He did as the angel said and called two of his servants and a trusted soldier to come to him. Cornelius told them everything that the angel had said to him. Then he sent the men off to the city of Joppa to find Peter.

The next day at about twelve noon, Peter went up on to the roof of Simon's house to pray. It was just as the men were coming near to the city of Joppa. Peter was hungry and wanted to eat something. As lunch was being made, Peter had a vision of the heavens being opened. He saw a large sheet being let down by its four corners to the ground. There were all kinds of animals and reptiles and birds in it. Peter then heard a voice that said to him, 'Get up, Peter, kill and eat.'

'No, Lord,' replied Peter. 'I have never eaten anything that is unclean. Your law does not allow it.'

Then the voice said, 'Do not call unclean what God has made clean, Peter.'

This happened three times and then the sheet was taken immediately back into heaven.

Peter was baffled about what it all meant. Meanwhile, the men that had been sent by Cornelius stood at the gate to Simon's house. They had asked people where they might find Peter who was staying there. While Peter was reflecting about the meaning of the vision, the Holy Spirit spoke to him. 'See, there are three men looking for you. Stand up and go down to them. Do not be reluctant to go with them, because I have sent them to you.'

So, Peter went down to the men. He said to them, 'I am the man you are looking for. Why have you come to see me?'

'Our master is Cornelius. He is a centurion. He is a good man who fears God. There is no one who has anything bad to say about him in all of Israel. An angel of the Lord told him to send for you. He wants you to come to his house. He will listen to what you have to tell him about God.'

When Peter heard this, he invited them into the house as his guests.

WHAT'S THE POINT:

In the Old Testament, God wanted his people, the Jews, to be different. He gave them laws to help them live in a different way to the other nations. But the differences meant that the good news of Jesus did not go from the first disciples who were Jewish, to the other nations who were Gentiles. God gives Peter a vision to show that the obstacles were no longer important. The good news of Jesus is for everyone!

LOOK BACK:

Read Mark 7:14-23

Jesus says that what makes us 'dirty' or 'unclean', has nothing to do with where we are from, what colour our skin is, or even what we eat. It is in our hearts.

THINK:

Does God accept everyone, no matter what they believe and what they do?

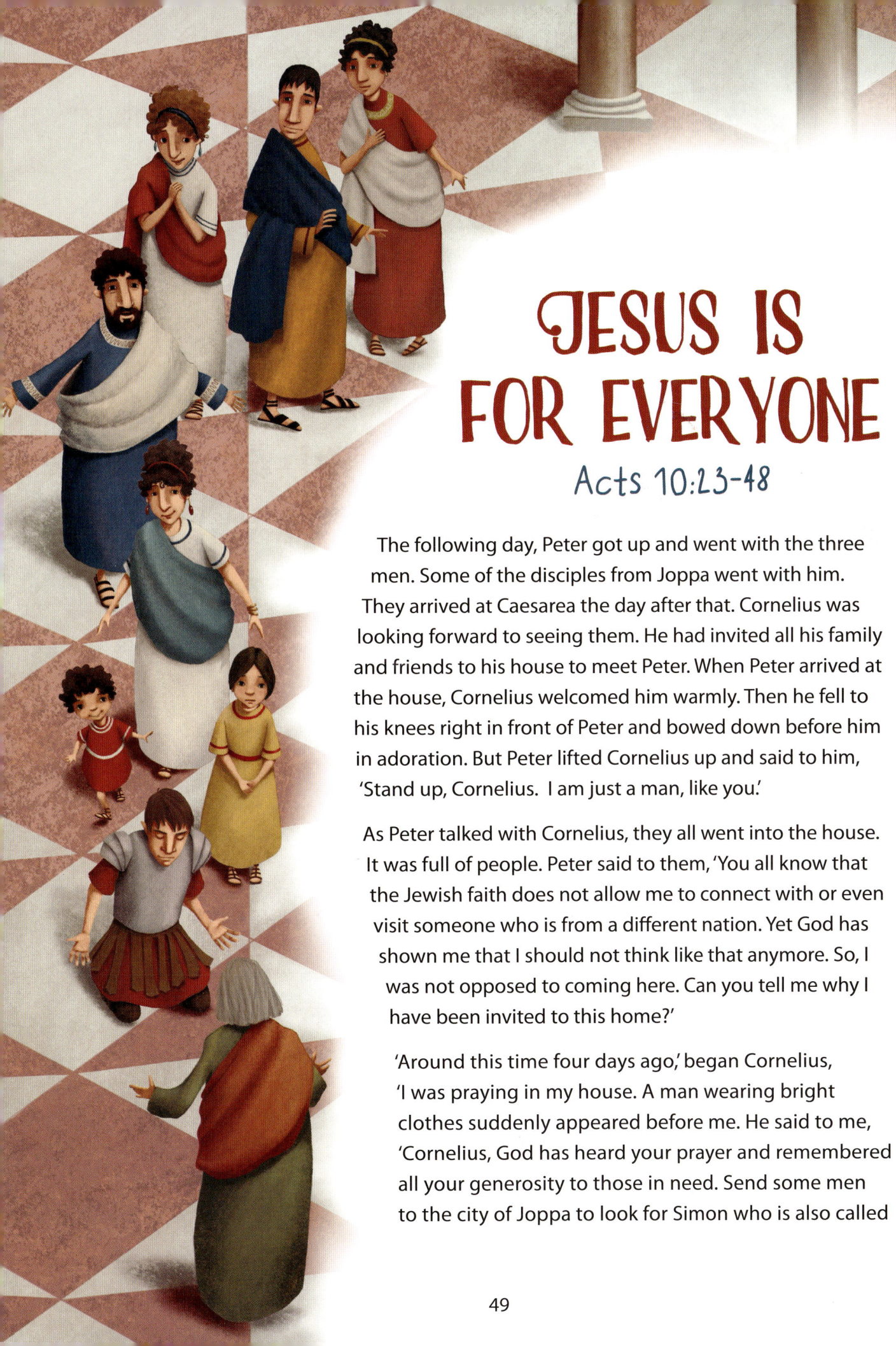

JESUS IS FOR EVERYONE

Acts 10:23-48

The following day, Peter got up and went with the three men. Some of the disciples from Joppa went with him. They arrived at Caesarea the day after that. Cornelius was looking forward to seeing them. He had invited all his family and friends to his house to meet Peter. When Peter arrived at the house, Cornelius welcomed him warmly. Then he fell to his knees right in front of Peter and bowed down before him in adoration. But Peter lifted Cornelius up and said to him, 'Stand up, Cornelius. I am just a man, like you.'

As Peter talked with Cornelius, they all went into the house. It was full of people. Peter said to them, 'You all know that the Jewish faith does not allow me to connect with or even visit someone who is from a different nation. Yet God has shown me that I should not think like that anymore. So, I was not opposed to coming here. Can you tell me why I have been invited to this home?'

'Around this time four days ago,' began Cornelius, 'I was praying in my house. A man wearing bright clothes suddenly appeared before me. He said to me, 'Cornelius, God has heard your prayer and remembered all your generosity to those in need. Send some men to the city of Joppa to look for Simon who is also called

49

Peter. He is staying at Simon the tanner's house by the sea.' So, I did what the angel told me and immediately sent for you. You have been very kind to come here to my home. Peter, we are all here in the presence of God to listen to what you have been commanded by the Lord to tell us.'

Then Peter said, 'I now truly understand that God is not biased. God accepts anyone who fears him and does what is right, and it doesn't matter what country they are from. The Word of God was sent to the Israelites. It proclaimed the good news of peace through Jesus Christ who is Lord of all. You heard what happened throughout the region of Judea. It started in Galilee after John the Baptist baptised Jesus in the River Jordan. He declared that God anointed Jesus of Nazareth with the Holy Spirit and with power.

Then Jesus went about doing good things. Because God was with him, Jesus healed anyone who felt crushed by the devil. We saw everything Jesus did in Jerusalem and surrounding areas where the Jews live. They killed him by hanging Jesus on a cross. But on the third day, God raised Jesus to life. Then Jesus appeared to those of us whom God had chosen to be witnesses of Christ's resurrection. We ate and drank with Jesus after he rose from the grave. Then Jesus commanded us to tell everyone that God has made him the judge of the living and the dead. All the prophets in the Scriptures tell us that anyone who believes in Jesus, will be forgiven their sins through his name.'

As Peter was speaking, the Holy Spirit came upon those who were listening to the Word of God. The Jewish believers, who were with Peter, were amazed at this because now the gift of the Holy Spirit was given to the Gentiles. They heard them speaking in languages that were not their own and praising God.

Peter then said, 'Who can stop these people from being baptised with water? They have received the Holy Spirit, just like us.' He commanded that all the people in the home of Cornelius be baptised with water in the name of Jesus Christ. He was then asked to stay with them for a number of days.

WHAT'S THE POINT:

God told Peter to stop thinking that the Gentiles were 'unclean'. Peter learned that God has no favourites! Cornelius was a good and kind man. He helped the poor. People thought well of him. But Cornelius did not know Jesus. He needed to hear the gospel – that Jesus Christ died on the cross for him; and that Jesus Christ is Saviour, Lord, and Judge – not only for Cornelius, but for everyone! We all must put our faith in Jesus and be saved!

WHAT IS THE GOSPEL?

How does Peter explain the good news of Jesus to Cornelius?
Can you think of his main points? Read Acts 10:36-43 again.

ACTS 10:36-39:	THE _____ OF JESUS.
ACTS 10:39:	THE _____ OF JESUS.
ACTS 10:40-41:	THE _____ OF JESUS.
ACTS 10:42:	JESUS IS THE _____.
ACTS 10:43:	WE MUST _____ JESUS.

If you were to write down one thing that Jesus commands us to tell our friends, what would you write? Would it be Acts 10:42?

THINK:

What happened to Cornelius and his household as Peter told them about Jesus, is the Gentile version of what happened at Pentecost to the Jewish believers! Can you think what it means?

REMEMBER:

The Word of God and the Holy Spirit of God together do the work of God!

NO ONE LEFT OUT

Acts 11:1-18

The apostles and other disciples in Judea heard the wonderful news that the Gentiles had received the Word of God as well. When Peter made his way to Jerusalem, some Jewish believers there criticised him. 'Peter, you went to the Gentiles and ate with them!' they exclaimed.

But Peter told them what happened. 'I was praying in Joppa when I had a vision of what looked like a large sheet coming down from heaven. It was held by each corner, and it came to rest before me. I looked at it very carefully. I saw different types of animals and reptiles and birds on it. Then I heard a voice which said to me, "Peter, get up, kill something and eat it." But I said, "No way Lord! I have never eaten anything that your law does not allow." Then the voice said, "Do not call unclean anything that God has made clean." This happened three times!' exclaimed Peter. 'After that it was taken back up to heaven. All of a sudden there were three men at Simon's door looking for me. They had travelled all the way from Caesarea. The Holy Spirit told me to go with them and not to worry that they were Gentiles. These six disciples of Jesus went with me,' he said, pointing to the men, 'and when we got there, we went in to the man's house. The man told us that he had seen an angel standing in his house, who said to him, "Send some men to the city of Joppa and have them bring back Simon, who is also called Peter. He will tell you good news about Jesus Christ. You and your family will be saved by this gospel." When I started to speak the gospel of Jesus, the Holy Spirit came upon everyone in the house, just as he did with us in the beginning. Then I remembered what the Lord had said – "John baptised with water, but you will be baptised with the Holy Spirit." Well then, if God gave them the same gift that he gave us when we believed in the Lord Jesus Christ, who was I to stand in God's way?'

When they heard Peter's account of what happened, they said nothing for a moment. But then, they began to praise God. 'Clearly God has allowed the Gentiles to receive the gift of repentance that leads to life, as well!' they exclaimed.

WHAT'S THE POINT:

Peter gets into all sorts of trouble with the believers in Jerusalem because he brought the gospel of Jesus to the home of the Gentile, Cornelius. They were astonished when they heard what had happened from Peter – the Gentiles received God's Spirit in the same way as the Jews and therefore should be baptised. Everyone who believes in Jesus are equal and are united in Jesus.

LOOK BACK:

Read Genesis 12:3

The Jewish believers in Jerusalem thought that Peter had done something wrong. Perhaps they had forgotten God's promise to bless all the families of the earth.

CHECK IT OUT:

Read 1 Corinthians 12:12-13

Think of your body – you have different limbs and organs. Your body only works when your different parts work together. In a similar way the church is to be like a body with everyone working together and united as one body.

THINK:

How will people from other cultures and religions hear the gospel of Jesus Christ?

TIME TO GROW

Acts 11:19-30

After Stephen was killed, fierce persecution began against those who loved the Lord Jesus. Many travelled from Jerusalem to other places for safety, as far away as Phoenicia, Cyprus, and Antioch. They only spoke the Word of God to the Jews. Some men of Cyprus and Cyrene arrived at Antioch. They preached about the Lord Jesus to the **Hellenists**. The Lord's hand was upon them. There was a large number of people who turned to follow the Lord Jesus. The church in Jerusalem heard about this and sent Barnabas to Antioch. He saw the **grace** of God at work in the lives of the people and he was very glad. He encouraged

all of them to focus on the Lord and stay faithful to him. Barnabas was a good man. He was full of the Holy Spirit. He was full of faith in Jesus Christ. Many people were added to the Lord's church.

Then Barnabas went to the city of Tarsus in search of Saul. When he found him, Barnabas brought Saul back to the city of Antioch. They spent a year there with the church and taught the Scriptures to many people. The disciples were first called Christians in Antioch.

At that time, some prophets arrived in Antioch from Jerusalem. One of the prophets was called Agabus. By the Spirit of God, Agabus predicted that there would be a bad famine all over the world (this would happen in the days of the Roman Emperor, Claudius). The disciples decided that anyone who had the means, should send aid to the brothers in Christ living in the region of Judea. And that is what they did. They told Barnabas and Saul to give the aid to the elders of Judea and sent them on their way.

WHAT'S THE POINT:

God grows his church by scattering his people out of their comfort zones. They speak the gospel of Jesus as they go. The seed of God's Word is spread, and more people become Christians. God grows his church by gathering his people together. Saul and Barnabas gather with the Christians and teach them. This is how God builds up his people. God grows his church by sending people and gifts to do his work.

LOOK FORWARD:

Read 1 Corinthians 3:6

Paul tells us that only God grows the church. If the apostle Paul can't grow churches, neither can we!

THINK:

Through the difficulty and suffering of his people, God does something truly amazing – can you think what it is? Read Acts 11:19-21 again to help you.

PRAY AND TRUST
Acts 12:1-19

Around that time, King Herod reached out to kill some of the disciples of Jesus. He had James the brother of John killed with the sword. When he saw that his death made the Jewish people happy, King Herod went on to arrest Peter. This happened during the Feast of Unleavened Bread. When Peter was arrested, he was thrown into prison. There were four squads of soldiers ordered to guard him. King Herod intended to bring Peter out to the people and execute him, when the Passover had finished. So, Peter was kept in prison. The church earnestly prayed to God for him.

When it was time for Herod to bring Peter out to the people, that very same night, Peter was sleeping between two guards. He was bound by two chains. There were sentries outside guarding the prison. Suddenly an angel of the Lord stood beside Peter. The prison cell was filled with light. The angel struck Peter's side to wake him up. 'Get up, quickly,' the angel said. Peter's chains fell off his hands. The angel said, 'Get dressed and put your sandals on.' Peter did what he was told to do. Then the angel said, 'Wrap your robe around you and follow me.'

Peter went out and followed the angel. Peter was half-asleep and did not know if what was happening was real. He thought he was seeing a vision. When they had passed the first and second guard, they came to the iron gate that led into the city. It opened by itself. They went out and passed on through one street. All of a sudden, the angel departed from him. Then Peter became fully aware of what had just happened. 'Now I know, without a doubt, that the Lord sent his angel and delivered me from the hand of Herod and from all that the Jewish people intended,' he said to himself.

As soon as he understood what had happened, Peter went to Mary's house. She was the mother of John, also called Mark. Many people had gathered in her home to pray. When Peter knocked on the gateway door, a servant girl came to answer it. Her name was Rhoda. As she approached, she recognised Peter's voice. She was so overcome with joy that she turned around and went back in to tell the others that Peter was at the gate.

'You are mad in the head,' they said to Rhoda. But she insisted that Peter was at the gate. 'It must be his angel!' they exclaimed.

Meanwhile, Peter kept knocking at the gateway door. When they opened it, they were astonished to see Peter standing before them. Peter motioned with his hand to be quiet.

Then he told them how the Lord got him out of prison. 'Tell James (the brother of Jesus) and the other brothers and sisters about this,' Peter said. Then he left them and went to another place so he wouldn't be captured again.

As soon as he understood what had happened, Peter went to Mary's house. She was the mother of John, also called Mark. Many people had gathered in her home to pray. When Peter knocked on the door, a servant girl came to answer it. Her name was Rhoda. As she approached, she recognised Peter's voice. She was so overcome with joy that she turned around and went back in to tell the others that Peter was outside. 'You are mad in the head,' they said to Rhoda. But she insisted that Peter was at the door. 'It must be his angel!' they exclaimed. Meanwhile, Peter kept knocking. When they finally opened the door, they were astonished to see Peter standing before them. Peter motioned with his hand to be quiet.

WHAT'S THE POINT:

Herod thought he was God. He had power. He had the Roman Empire supporting him. From his heights, he dished out death to the church. But Herod was brought down low by God. Herod did not give glory to God, and he was eaten by worms. God is more powerful than Herod. God is more powerful than any human government. So, when you are persecuted for loving and following Jesus, pray and trust God.

LOOK FORWARD:

Read 2 Corinthians 10:3-5

We have weapons to fight against sin, the world, and the devil. They are love, faith, and hope in Jesus Christ, prayer, and the Bible.

CHECK THIS OUT:

Read Acts 6:7, 9:31 and 12:24 again

The way we show that we believe in God is that we pray, and we keep telling others about Jesus. Remember it is God who gives the growth!

THINK:

What should be the *first* thing you do for Christians who are persecuted for their faith in Jesus? Read Acts 12:5 again to help you.

THE FIRST MISSION
Acts 13:1-12

In the church at Antioch were certain prophets and teachers, Barnabas, Simeon who also called Niger, Lucius of Cyrene, Manaen who had been brought up with Herod the governor, and Saul who was also called Paul. One day as they were serving the Lord and fasting, the Holy Spirit said, 'Set Barnabas and Paul aside for the work that I have called them to do.'

When they had finished fasting and praying, they placed their hands on the two men and sent them away. So, Barnabas and Paul were sent by the Holy Spirit to travel down to the port city of Seleucia. From there they sailed to Cyprus.

As soon as they arrived in Salamis, they preached the Word of God in the Jewish synagogues. John was there to help them. They proclaimed the good news about Jesus

throughout the island. When they arrived at Paphos, they met a magician called Bar-Jesus, who was also known as Elymas. He was a Jew and a false prophet. He was with a Roman official called Sergius Paulus, who was known to be a clever man. Sergius Paulus invited Barnabas and Paul to come to him, so that he might hear the Word of God from them. However, Elymas the magician was against them. He tried to turn Sergius Paulus away from the truth of the gospel. Filled with the Holy Spirit, Paul looked at him closely and said, 'You son of the devil. You are an enemy of all that is pure and right. You are full of treachery and corruption. Will you not stop distorting the straight path of the Lord? But now, the hand of the Lord is on you. For a while, you will be blind. You will not be able to see the sun.' As soon as Paul had said this, mist and darkness came upon Elymas. He could not see. He had to ask people to lead him by the hand when he wanted to go anywhere. When Sergius Paulus saw what had happened to Elymas, he believed in the Lord. He was amazed at the Lord's teaching.

WHAT'S THE POINT:

God wanted the good news about his Son Jesus to spread throughout the world. Paul and Barnabas were sent to Cyprus to tell people about Jesus. Elymas the magician opposed and twisted the message to stop people believing in Jesus. Paul challenged him and Elymas was struck blind. God does not act this way every time someone is against him. But it shows that nothing will stop the good news of Jesus going to every corner of God's world.

LOOK BACK:

Read John 16:3, and Matthew 28:19

Jesus wants us to take his gospel to new people in new places. Sometimes there will be opposition and it can make us feel afraid. But Jesus is with us. Nothing will stop his gospel from going into his world.

THINK:

Elymas was struck blind for opposing the gospel. It is a miracle of judgement. This is the third negative miracle in the book of Acts. Can you remember what the others are?

PROMISES TO KEEP

Acts 13:13-52

Paul and Barnabas set sail again and travelled from Paphos to the mainland cities of Perga in Pamphylia and Antioch in Pisidia. They were at Antioch on the **Sabbath** day. They went into the synagogue and sat down. After the reading of the Law and the Prophets, the synagogue rulers sent word to them. 'If you have anything to preach to the people, then say it,' they said. Then Paul stood up and motioned with his hand to quieten the people. He reminded the people who had gathered about the history of Israel, and he spoke of Jesus the Messiah.

'Men of Israel,' he began, 'and all of you who fear God, listen to me. The God of the people of Israel chose our fathers and gave strength to our people when they lived in the land of Egypt. With great power, God delivered them from their oppressors. For about forty years the Lord looked after them in the wilderness. When he had destroyed seven nations in the land of Canaan, he divided the land between them. All this took about four hundred and fifty years. Then God gave them judges until Samuel the prophet.

'The people of Israel wanted a king to rule them. So, God gave them Saul, the son of Kish of the tribe of Benjamin. King Saul reigned for forty years.

God raised
up David to
replace Saul as
king. God said, 'I
have found David,
the son of Jesse, to
be a man after my own
heart. He shall do my will.'
From David's offspring and
according to his own promises,
God has raised a Saviour for Israel.
He is called Jesus. This Saviour, and this
word of salvation, is sent to you and to
all who fear God.'

The following Sabbath nearly the whole city came
together to hear Barnabas and Paul preach the Word
of God to them. But the Jews were jealous and opposed
their message. They tried to contradict Paul and Barnabas as
they spoke the gospel to the people. The two men continued
to speak boldly, saying, 'The Lord gave us this command: "I have
made you a light to the Gentiles, that you should work for the
saving of souls to the ends of the earth."'

When the Gentiles heard the gospel message, they were filled with joy
and believed. The word of the Lord spread throughout the whole area.
But the Jews stirred up the leaders of the city against Barnabas and Paul,
who sent them away. Therefore, Barnabas and Paul left the city of Antioch
and travelled to Iconium.

WHAT'S THE POINT:

Paul told the people that Jesus is the Saviour that God promised from the Old Testament. Hatred and jealousy filled the Jews. They were blinded to the truth about Jesus, and the salvation that Jesus offers to anyone who trusts him. Jealousy ruins relationships, especially the relationship that everyone so desperately needs with the Lord and Saviour, Jesus Christ.

LOOK BACK:

Read Isaiah 49:6 and John 8:12

The task of God's Servant was to act as a light to the nations and to be the way of God's salvation throughout the world. The early Christians saw this passage fulfilled in Jesus. But the fact that Paul uses it here helps us see that followers of Jesus have a similar task, to make the light of the gospel of Jesus known to the whole world.

CHECK THIS OUT:

Read Galatians 5:22

The new group of disciples were filled with joy. The fruit of the Holy Spirit is joy. Sadly, this is not experienced by people who refuse to believe and follow Jesus.

THINK:

In Galatians 5, what else does Paul say the fruit of the Holy Spirit is?

HARD TIMES
Acts 14:1-28

Paul and Barnabas went together to the synagogue in Iconium. They spoke the Word of God to a great number of people and many Jews and Gentiles believed in the Lord Jesus. But those Jews who did not believe stirred up the Gentiles and corrupted their minds against Paul and Barnabas. The city was divided. There were some who supported the Jews and others who sided with the apostles. When an attempt was made to stone them, Paul and Barnabas were aware of it and fled to Lystra and Derbe, cities of Lycaonia and to the surrounding areas of the province of Galatia. They continued to preach the gospel there.

There was a man in Lystra who was crippled from birth and had never walked. He listened carefully to Paul as he spoke the Word of God. Paul looked at the crippled man intently. He could see that the man had the faith to be healed, so in a loud voice he said, 'Stand up on your feet!' Immediately the man leapt up and started to walk. When the people saw what Paul had done, in their own language they called out, 'The gods have become like men and come down to us!' They called Barnabas 'Zeus' and they called Paul 'Hermes' because he was the main speaker. The temple of Zeus was at the gates of the city. The priest of Zeus brought oxen and wreaths of flowers to the gates, to offer a sacrifice with the people. But when Paul and Barnabas heard of this, they tore their clothes and ran out into the crowds. They cried out, 'Why are you doing this? We are human beings, with feelings, just like you. We bring good news to all of you, that you should turn away from these empty and false things and turn to the true and living God. He made the heaven and the earth and the sea. He made everything that is in them. In the past, God let all people from every nation walk

in their own ways. He did not leave us without proof of himself. In his goodness, God gave us rain from heaven and seasons of plenty. God filled your hearts with food and happiness.' Even though the apostles had spoken these words to them, they barely prevented the people from sacrificing to them.

Some Jews came from Antioch and Iconium, who swayed the people. They stoned Paul and put him out of the city. They thought he was dead. However, when the disciples stood around him, Paul got up and went back into the city. The next day, Paul and Barnabas left for Derbe. When they had preached the gospel of Jesus to that city, they travelled back to Lystra, and to Iconium and to Antioch. They encouraged the disciples in these cities to keep following Christ Jesus. 'We must go through many hardships to enter the kingdom of God,' they said.

Then Paul and Barnabas travelled through Pisidia and on to Pamphylia. They preached the Word of God in Perga before heading to the port city of Attalia. Then they set sail for Antioch in Syria. When they arrived, they called the church together and told them everything that God had done with them. They told how God had made it possible for them to preach the gospel to the Gentiles. And they stayed a long time with the disciples there.

WHAT'S THE POINT:

The way that the gospel moves forward, and the risen Jesus brings salvation, is through preaching. When Paul preached the gospel, it divided people. And it brought others together for the first time. Paul warned new disciples that they will face many hard times in their lives. The Christian life is not easy. When difficulties come, we must look to Jesus and keep speaking about him.

CHECK THIS OUT:

Read 2 Timothy 3:10-13

It's amazing! Even though people tried to kill Paul, he kept boldly telling them about Jesus. One of the young men who came to faith in Jesus when Paul preached at Lystra was called Timothy. Paul reminded Timothy of that visit in his second letter to him, and of the certainty of persecution for anyone who wants to live a life that pleases Jesus. How do you feel about that?

THINK:

Is it possible to serve Christ and at the same time be at peace with the world? Read James 4:4 to help you.

CHRISTIAN FOCUS PUBLICATIONS

Christian Focus Publications publishes books for adults and children under its four main imprints: Christian Focus, CF4K, Mentor and Christian Heritage. Our books reflect our conviction that God's Word is reliable and Jesus is the way to know him, and live for ever with him.

Our children's publication list covers pre-school to early teens. We also publish personal and family devotional titles, biographies and inspirational stories that children will love.

From pre-school board books to teenage apologetics, we have it covered!

Christian Focus Publications Ltd, Geanies House, Fearn, Ross-shire, IV20 1TW, Scotland, United Kingdom.

www.christianfocus.com

CHRISTIAN FOCUS PUBLICATIONS

Christian Focus | Christian Heritage | CF4K | Mentor